Sanjeev Kapoor's

Kadai Cooking

Sanjeev Kapoor's

Kadai Cooking

In association with Alyona Kapoor

www.popularprakashan.com

Published by
POPULAR PRAKASHAN PVT. LTD.
301, Mahalaxmi Chambers
22, Bhulabhai Desai Road
Mumbai - 400 026
for KHANA KHAZANA PUBLICATIONS PVT. LTD.

© 2008 Sanjeev Kapoor
First Published 2008
First Reprint April 2008
Second Reprint 2009

WORLD RIGHTS RESERVED. The contents – all recipes, photographs and drawings are original and copyrighted. No portion of this book shall be reproduced, stored in a retrieval system or transmitted by any means, electronic, mechanical, photocopying, recording or otherwise, without the written permission of the author and the publisher.

(4106)
ISBN 978-81-7991-358-1

Photography: Bharat Bhirangi

PRINTED IN INDIA
Abhinav Prints
K-37, Udyog Nagar
Industrial Area, Delhi- 40

You don't have to cook fancy or
complicated masterpieces - just good food from fresh ingredients.

Julia Child

Author's note

The *Kadai* is a versatile piece of kitchen equipment which is found in every Indian home. Used for deep-frying, stir-frying, steaming or cooking foods with minimum water and oil, no kitchen would be complete without a well-used *kadai*.

With its round bottom and sloping sides it is similar to the Chinese wok and the Northwest Frontier balti of recent fame. Made of cast iron, a metal that retains and evenly distributes heat, the *kadai* is particularly useful for stir-frying dishes over high heat (*bhuna*) and for cooking foods which can cook in their own juices or in thick gravies. So ubiquitous is its use in North India that a whole new method of cooking has developed around the *kadai*, making *kadai* cooking a specialised form of Indian cooking.

Here are some tips for successful *kadai*-cooking.

- Buy a *kadai* made of cast–iron, carbon steel or thick aluminium. Non-stick *kadais* are also available. The bottom of the *kadai* should be much thicker than the sides.
- To season a new *kadai*, wash it out well with detergent. Heat the *kadai* over a high heat till smoking. Swirl around two tablespoons of oil around the entire inner surface. Remove from heat and carefully spread the oil over the inside surface of the *kadai* with a paper towel or pieces of muslin. Repeat the process a few times.

- Place a special metal ring on the gas stove meant to hold the *kadai* firmly in place while cooking.
- Use tongs or thick pot holders to handle a hot *kadai*.
- Food served directly from the *kadai* is not only hotter and more flavoursome, but also presents a delightful ethnic touch.
- Wash the *kadai* well after each use.

While most of the recipes included in this book are from North India, where kadai-cooking is a fine art, I have included recipes from across our culinary diverse country, where the *kadai* also has a special place. However, I have not included recipes for deep-frying as, for the purposes of this book, *kadai*-cooking implies cooking with minimum liquid and fat. There are recipes in here for every course in a meal from spicy snacks and starters through vegetarian and non-vegetarian main courses to desserts. As usual, every recipe has been tried and tested to perfection and serves four persons.

I hope you will enjoy this book and create many happy meals for yourself and your family with this multi-purpose utensil!

Happy Cooking!

Acknowledgements

Afsheen Panjwani
Anand Bhandiwad
Anil Bhandari
Anupa Das
Ashwini Patwardhan
Bharati Anand
Bhartendu Sharma
Drs. Meena and Ram Prabhoo
Gajendra Mule
Ganesh Pednekar
Harpal Singh Sokhi
Jayadeep Chaubal
Jyotsna and Mayur Dvivedi
Kalpana Deshmukh
Lohana Khaandaan

Mahendra Ghanekar
Mrs. Lata Lohana and
Capt. K. K. Lohana
Namrata and Sanjiv Bahl
Neelima Acharya
Neena Murdeshwar
Pooja and Rajeev Kapoor
Rajeev Matta
Rita D'Souza
Rutika Samtani
Saurabh Mishra
Smeeta Bhatkal
Tripta Bhagattjee
Trupti Kale
Vinayak Gawande

Contents

Main Course - Non-Vegetarian

Kadai Chicken	67
Murg Ka Mokal	69
Kadai Gosht Hussainee	71
Narial Ka Gosht	74
Dahi Ka Keema	76
Surmai With Tomatoes	78
Gosht Gulburga	81
Kekda Curry	83
Kadai Prawns	86
Methi Murg	88

Rice

Makai Palak Pulao	90
Chicken Keema Pulao	93
Chutney Pulao	95
Phodnicha Bhaat	97

Desserts

Moong Dal Halwa	99
Sooji Aur Badam Ka Halwa	100
Kalakand	102
Saeb Ka Halwa	104

TIL JHINGA

24 (250 grams) medium prawns
$\frac{1}{3}$ cup sesame seeds (*til*)
1 teaspoon garlic paste
1 teaspoon ginger paste
$\frac{1}{4}$ teaspoon white pepper powder
salt to taste
2 tablespoons lemon juice
2 tablespoons drained yogurt
$\frac{1}{2}$ cup grated processed cheese

$\frac{1}{2}$ teaspoon carom seeds (*ajwain*)
2 tablespoons cream
$\frac{1}{2}$ teaspoon mace-cardamom powder
$1\frac{1}{2}$ tablespoons powdered roasted split Bengal gram (*chana dal*)
1 cup breadcrumbs
oil for deep-frying
2 lemons, cut into wedges
green chutney, to serve

1. Peel and devein the prawns, leaving the tails intact. Pat the prawns dry. Mix together the garlic paste, ginger paste, white pepper powder, salt and lemon juice. Rub the paste all over the prawns and set aside for half an hour. Squeeze the prawns lightly to remove excess moisture and set aside.

2. Whisk together the drained yogurt and cheese till smooth. Add the carom seeds, cream, mace-cardamom powder and powdered roasted *chana dal*. Coat the prawns with the mixture and set aside for half an hour.

3. Mix the breadcrumbs and sesame seeds on a plate. Roll the prawns in the mixture and refrigerate for about fifteen minutes.

4. Heat the oil in a *kadai* and deep-fry the prawns over medium heat for about four or five minutes. Drain and set aside for four or five minutes.

5. Deep-fry again for two or three minutes. Drain on absorbent paper.

6. Serve hot with lemon wedges and green chutney.

Til Jhinga

PRAWN BHUNA

500 grams king prawns, peeled and deveined

2 teaspoons white vinegar

3 green chillies, chopped

2 teaspoons red chilli powder

¾ teaspoon turmeric powder

salt to taste

1 teaspoon garlic paste

4 tablespoons oil

2 large onions, grated

2 dried red chillies, seeded and sliced

1 large tomato, chopped

1 tablespoon lemon juice

½ teaspoon *garam masala* powder

2 tablespoons chopped fresh coriander leaves

1. Marinate the prawns in a mixture of the vinegar, green chillies, one teaspoon chilli powder, turmeric powder, salt and garlic paste for ten minutes.

2. Heat the oil in a *kadai;* add the onions and sauté for three or four minutes till golden brown.

3. Add the remaining chilli powder and red chillies and sauté for one minute. Add the tomato and cook till soft. Add the prawns and cook for two or three minutes. Add half a cup of water and cook for another five minutes.

4. Stir in the lemon juice and *garam masala* powder. Serve hot, garnished with coriander leaves.

KADAK BHINDI

500 grams ladies' fingers (*bhindi*)
3 tablespoons oil
a pinch of asafoetida (*hing*)
½ teaspoon cumin seeds
1 medium onion, sliced
salt to taste

½ teaspoon red chilli powder
1 teaspoon coriander powder
½ teaspoon *garam masala* powder
¼ teaspoon dried mango powder *(amchur)*
2 tablespoons chopped fresh coriander
leaves

1. Cut the *bhindi* into one-and-a-half-inch long diagonal pieces.

2. Heat the oil in a *kadai;* add the asafoetida and cumin seeds. When they begin to change colour, add the onion. Sauté till light brown. Add the *bhindi* and cook, stirring continuously, over low heat till lightly browned.

3. Sprinkle the salt, chilli powder, coriander powder, *garam masala* powder and *amchur* over the *bhindi* and toss well. Cook for one minute longer. Serve immediately, garnished with coriander leaves.

Kadai Cooking

TIL MOONGFALLI ALOO

750 grams baby potatoes

1 tablespoon sesame seeds (*til*)

2 tablespoons peanuts, coarsely crushed

salt to taste

3 tablespoons oil

1 teaspoon cumin seeds

4 green chillies, chopped

1 inch ginger, chopped

1 tablespoon garlic paste

1 teaspoon roasted cumin powder

1 teaspoon red chilli powder

1½ tablespoons grated fresh coconut

1 teaspoon *garam masala* powder

2 teaspoons lemon juice

2 tablespoons chopped fresh coriander leaves

1. Parboil the unpeeled potatoes in salted water and set aside. Press them lightly.
2. Heat the oil in a *kadai*; add the cumin seeds, green chillies and ginger. When the seeds begin to change colour, add the garlic paste and sauté for two or three minutes. Add the potatoes and toss well.
3. Add the sesame seeds, peanuts, roasted cumin powder, chilli powder, coconut and *garam masala* powder. Adjust salt.
4. Continue to cook for five minutes, tossing continuously. Stir in the lemon juice.
5. Serve hot, garnished with coriander leaves.

 Til Moongfalli Aloo

KHADA MASALA CHICKEN

800 grams boneless chicken,
cut into cubes

4 tablespoons oil

2 bay leaves

¼ teaspoon mustard seeds

¼ teaspoon fennel seeds (*saunf*)

¼ teaspoon onion seeds (*kalonji*)

2 dried red chillies, crushed

½ teaspoon cumin seeds

¼ teaspoon fenugreek seeds (*methi dana*)

½ teaspoon dried pomegranate
seeds (*anardana*), crushed

1 inch ginger, grated

5-6 cloves garlic, sliced

1 large onion, sliced

4 green chillies, slit

1 medium tomato, sliced

salt to taste

1 tablespoon chopped fresh
coriander leaves

Kadai Cooking

1. Heat the oil in a *kadai*; add the bay leaves, mustard seeds, fennel seeds, onion seeds, crushed red chillies, cumin seeds, fenugreek seeds and pomegranate seeds.

2. When they begin to change colour, add the ginger and garlic. Sauté for half a minute and add the onion and green chillies; sauté over medium heat till the onion turns light brown.

3. Add the chicken, tomato and salt and sauté over medium heat, stirring occasionally, for eight to ten minutes till the chicken is almost done. Lower the heat, cover and cook for five or six minutes longer.

4. Garnish with coriander leaves and serve hot.

SPICY LAMB TIKKA

600 grams boneless lamb, cut into cubes

2 tablespoons unripe green
  papaya paste

3 tablespoons yogurt

1 teaspoon ginger paste

1 teaspoon garlic paste

1 teaspoon red chilli powder

¼ teaspoon turmeric powder

2 teaspoons coriander powder

1 teaspoon roasted cumin powder

salt to taste

2 tablespoons lemon juice

1 tablespoon chopped fresh
  coriander leaves

2 tablespoons oil

2 lemons, cut into wedges

2 large onions, cut into rings

1. Rub the papaya paste into the lamb cubes and marinate for at least three hours, preferably in a refrigerator.

2. Mix together the yogurt, ginger paste, garlic paste, chilli powder, turmeric powder, coriander powder, roasted cumin powder, salt, lemon juice and coriander leaves. Marinate the lamb cubes in this mixture for twenty minutes.

3. Heat the oil in a *kadai* and sauté the lamb for four or five minutes. Add one cup of water and cook over medium heat till tender.

4 Garnish with lemon wedges and onion rings and serve immediately.

CHATPATA CHIWDA

250 grams nylon *poha*

4 tablespoons oil

25 curry leaves

3 green chillies, broken into bits

1 tablespoon sesame seeds (*til*)

½ cup peanuts

2 tablespoons roasted *chana dal*

¼ cup thinly sliced dried coconut (*khopra*)

½ teaspoon turmeric powder

½ teaspoon red chilli powder

2 tablespoons powdered sugar

salt to taste

1. Dry-roast the *poha* in a *kadai* over medium heat till crisp. Transfer to a bowl and set aside.

2. Heat the oil in the same *kadai*; add the curry leaves, green chillies, sesame seeds, peanuts, roasted *chana dal* and dried coconut and sauté over low heat till they change colour. Stir in the turmeric powder and chilli powder. Add the *poha* and mix gently so that the *poha* flakes do not break.

3. Sprinkle powdered sugar and salt and mix well. Remove from heat and set aside to cool. Place in an airtight jar. This *chiwda* has a long shelf life.

Chatpata Chiwda

CHICKEN 65

450 grams boneless chicken, cut into
  1½-inch pieces

½ cup yogurt

1½ tablespoons lemon juice

2 tablespoons rice flour

salt to taste

4 tablespoons oil

Masala

4 dried red chillies

2 inches ginger

6 garlic cloves

2 tablespoons coriander seeds

12-15 black peppercorns

1. Grind the ingredients for the *masala* to a fine paste.
2. Mix the yogurt, lemon juice, rice flour, salt and two tablespoons oil into the ground *masala* paste.
3. Coat the chicken with the *masala* paste and marinate for an hour in a refrigerator.

4. Heat the remaining oil in a thick-bottomed *kadai;* add the chicken pieces in small batches of six to eight pieces and stir-fry over high heat for one minute, tossing continuously. Add another batch of the chicken and repeat.

5. Lower heat once all the chicken has been added. Turn the pieces frequently, basting with the remaining *masala*.

6. Cook till the oil separates and the chicken turns crispy on the outside, but moist and soft on the inside.

7. Adjust salt, toss well and remove. Drain and serve hot.

Chef's Tip: If you use the chicken on the bone, it will be more succulent and tasty.

CHETTINAAD FRIED CHICKEN

1 whole (800 grams) chicken
2 medium onions, roughly chopped
1 inch ginger, roughly chopped
4-6 garlic cloves, roughly chopped
4 green chillies, roughly chopped
4-6 dried red chillies

½ teaspoon turmeric powder
1 tablespoon lemon juice
2 tablespoons rice flour
salt to taste
10-12 curry leaves, finely shredded
oil for shallow-frying

1. Split the chicken through the backbone and the breast, into two equal halves. Make three or four half-inch deep cuts on the breast and leg pieces.

2. Grind the onions, ginger, garlic, green chillies and red chillies with a little water to a smooth paste.

3. Mix the turmeric powder, lemon juice, rice flour and salt into the *masala* paste.

 Chettinaad Fried Chicken

4. Coat the chicken liberally with the paste and leave to marinate for two or three hours, preferably in a refrigerator. Mix the shredded curry leaves into the chicken.

5. Heat the oil in a *kadai*; add the marinated chicken and sauté over high heat for two minutes on both sides to seal the juices.

6. Lower heat to medium, cover with a lid and cook for fifteen to twenty minutes, turning over and basting frequently with the remaining marinade. Sprinkle a little water if the chicken starts drying out.

7. Cook over high heat for the last few minutes, so that the surface of the chicken is crisp and golden brown.

8. Cut into smaller pieces and serve hot.

KADAI VEGETABLES

10-12 French beans, cut into ¼-inch pieces

2 medium carrots, cut into ¼-inch cubes

¼ medium cauliflower, separated into florets

¼ cup shelled green peas

2 medium green capsicums, cut into ¼-inch pieces

1 tablespoon coriander seeds

1 teaspoon cumin seeds

4-5 dried red chillies

12-15 garlic cloves

3-4 green chillies

2 inches ginger

4 tablespoons oil

2 medium onions, sliced

½ teaspoon turmeric powder

1 tablespoon coriander powder

1 teaspoon red chilli powder

3 large tomatoes, roughly chopped

salt to taste

1 teaspoon *garam masala* powder

3 tablespoons chopped fresh coriander leaves

1. Grind the coriander, cumin seeds and three red chillies coarsely.
2. Grind the garlic, green chillies and half the ginger to a paste. Cut the remaining ginger into thin strips.
3. Heat the oil in a *kadai*. Add the coarsely ground spice powder and sauté for a while. Add the onions and sauté till golden brown.
4. Add the garlic-green chilli-ginger paste and sauté for one minute. Add all the vegetables, except the capsicums, and stir. Cook, covered over low heat, till the carrots are almost tender. Sprinkle a little water if necessary.
5. Add the turmeric powder, coriander powder and chilli powder and stir-fry continuously. Add the tomatoes, salt and half a cup of water and cook till the vegetables are cooked and the water has dried up.
6. Add the capsicums and cook for four or five minutes over low heat. Sprinkle with *garam masala* powder. Serve hot, garnished with ginger strips and coriander leaves.

KHUMB HARA DHANIA

600 grams fresh button mushrooms, trimmed

1 cup chopped fresh coriander leaves

2 tablespoons oil

5 green cardamoms

1 black cardamom

5 cloves

1 inch stick cinnamon

1 bay leaf

a pinch of mace (*javitri*)

$^2/_3$ cup boiled onion paste

4 teaspoons ginger paste

4 teaspoons garlic paste

4 green chillies, chopped

1 teaspoon red chilli powder

½ teaspoon coriander powder

1½ cups yogurt, whisked

salt to taste

3 tablespoons cashew nut paste

1½ inches ginger, cut into thin strips

Main Course - Vegetarian

1. Blanch the mushrooms in hot water for two minutes. Drain.

2. Heat the oil in a *kadai*; add the green and black cardamoms, cloves, cinnamon, bay leaf and mace and sauté over medium heat till fragrant.

3. Add the boiled onion paste and sauté for two or three minutes. Add the ginger and garlic pastes and continue to sauté for a while. Add the green chillies and sauté for half a minute.

4. Add the chilli powder and coriander powder and stir for half a minute.

5. Remove from heat and stir in the yogurt and salt. Return the pan to the heat. Add around three-fourth cup of water and bring to a boil. Lower heat and simmer till the oil rises to the surface. Add the cashew nut paste and simmer for two or three minutes.

6. Add the mushrooms and three-fourth cup of coriander leaves and simmer for two or three minutes. Transfer to a serving dish and garnish with the remaining coriander leaves and ginger strips.

7. Serve hot with steamed rice or *rotis*.

 Khumb Hara Dhania

MASALA KHUMB

600 grams fresh button mushrooms, quartered

8 dried red chillies

3 teaspoons coriander seeds

1 tablespoon oil

1 teaspoon cumin seeds

2 medium onions, sliced

3 teaspoons garlic paste

4 large tomatoes, puréed

salt to taste

4 green chillies, chopped

2 inches ginger, chopped

2 teaspoons *garam masala* powder

½ cup chopped fresh coriander leaves

1. Roast and pound the dried red chillies and coriander seeds with a mortar and pestle to a coarse powder.

2. Heat one tablespoon of oil in a *kadai*. Add the cumin seeds, onions and garlic paste and sauté for one minute over medium heat. Add the powdered spices and sauté for half a minute.

3. Add the tomato purée and salt and sauté till the oil separates. Add the green chillies and ginger and continue to sauté for one minute. Add the mushrooms and salt and cook, stirring gently, for seven to eight minutes. Stir in the *garam masala* powder.

4. Garnish with coriander leaves and serve hot with *rotis*.

CORN AND SPINACH MALAI

2 cups corn kernels, boiled

4 medium bunches (1 kilogram) fresh spinach leaves (*palak*), blanched and puréed

4 tablespoons fresh cream (*malai*)

2 teaspoons oil

5 green chillies, chopped

6-8 garlic cloves, chopped

salt to taste

½ teaspoon *garam masala* powder

½ tablespoon lemon juice

1. Heat the oil in a *kadai;* add the green chillies and garlic and sauté for half a minute.
2. Add the spinach purée and salt and sauté over medium heat for two or three minutes.
3. Add the *garam masala* powder and lemon juice and simmer for one minute.
4. Stir in the corn and serve hot, garnished with cream.

MUSHROOM BALCHAO

600 grams fresh button mushrooms,
   quartered
10-12 dried red chillies
8-10 garlic cloves
1 inch ginger
1 teaspoon cumin seeds
7-8 cloves
1 teaspoon mustard seeds

1 inch cinnamon
salt to taste
½ cup malt vinegar
2 tablespoons oil
2 medium onions, chopped
2 medium tomatoes, chopped
¾ cup tomato purée
1 tablespoon sugar

1. Grind the red chillies, garlic, ginger, cumin seeds, cloves, mustard seeds, cinnamon and salt with one-fourth cup of malt vinegar to a fine paste.

2. Heat the oil in a *kadai*; add the onions and sauté till light brown. Add the tomatoes, mix well and cook for five minutes, stirring continuously. Add the mushrooms, tomato purée and ground *masala* and cook for three or four minutes. Add the sugar and more salt if necessary and mix well. Add the remaining malt vinegar and cook for five to seven minutes. Serve hot.

BHARWAN KARELE

4 bitter gourds (*karela*)
salt to taste
1 tablespoon oil
1 medium onion, chopped
2 teaspoons ginger paste
1 tablespoon garlic paste
1 teaspoon coriander powder
½ teaspoon red chilli powder
1 teaspoon cumin powder
½ teaspoon turmeric powder
2 teaspoons tamarind juice

Stuffing
½ cup gram flour (*besan*)
1 medium onion, chopped
2 tablespoons chopped fresh
  coriander leaves
salt to taste
½ teaspoon red chilli powder
¼ teaspoon *garam masala* powder
1 teaspoon carom seeds (*ajwain*)

1. Scrape the bitter gourds; make a slit on one side and remove the seeds. Rub the salt over and inside the karele and set aside for one hour. Wash under running water and set aside.

2. For the stuffing, dry-roast the gram flour in a non-stick pan over low heat till fragrant. Remove from heat, transfer to a plate and set aside to cool. Add the onion, coriander leaves, salt, chilli powder, *garam masala* powder and carom seeds and mix well.

3. Stuff the *masala* mixture into each *karela* and set aside.

4. Heat the oil in a *kadai*; add the onion and sauté till light golden brown. Add the ginger paste and garlic paste and sauté for two minutes. Add the coriander powder, chilli powder, cumin powder and turmeric powder and mix well. Sauté the *masala* till fragrant.

5. Add the stuffed *karele*, half a cup of water and salt. Cover and cook over high heat for three or four minutes. Lower heat and cook for ten to twelve minutes, stirring gently at regular intervals. Add the tamarind juice and mix well. Cover once again and cook for another ten to fifteen minutes, or till the bitter gourds are cooked. Serve hot.

PUNJ RATNI DAL

2 tablespoons green gram (*sabut moong*)

2 tablespoons lentils (*sabut masoor*)

2 tablespoons black gram (*sabut urad*)

2 tablespoons split Bengal gram (*chana dal*)

2 tablespoons split pigeon peas
(*arhar dal/toovar dal*)

2 tablespoons pure *ghee*

1 medium onion, chopped

½ teaspoon red chilli powder

½ teaspoon turmeric powder

salt to taste

2 tablespoons white butter

¼ teaspoon *paanch phoron*

2 medium tomatoes, chopped

2 tablespoons yogurt, whisked

½ teaspoon *garam masala* powder

2 tablespoons chopped fresh coriander
leaves

1. Soak the *dals* in two cups of water for one hour. Drain and pressure-cook with three cups of water till soft.

2. Heat the *ghee* in a thick-bottomed *kadai*; add the onion and sauté till light brown. Stir in the chilli powder and turmeric powder.

3. Add the cooked *dals* and salt to taste. Mash lightly with the back of a ladle. Continue to cook, stirring continuously, for two or three minutes.

4. Heat the white butter in a separate *kadai*; add the *paanch phoron*, tomatoes, yogurt and *garam masala* powder and sauté over medium heat till the fat separates.

5. Add the mixture to the *dals* and simmer, stirring occasionally, for two or three minutes.

6. Serve hot, garnished with coriander leaves.

Note: *Paanch phoron* is a mixture of equal quantities of mustard seeds, cumin seeds, fenugreek seeds (*methi dana*), fennel seeds (*saunf*) and onion seeds (*kalonji*).

 Kadai Cooking

DAL AMRITSARI

½ cup split Bengal gram (*chana dal*)
½ cup split black gram (*chilkewali urad dal*)
salt to taste
¼ teaspoon turmeric powder
1 inch ginger, chopped
3 green chillies, chopped
2-3 tablespoons pure *ghee*

1 tablespoon butter
1 teaspoon cumin seeds
1 medium onion, chopped
2 medium tomatoes, chopped
½ teaspoon red chilli powder
1 tablespoon chopped fresh
   coriander leaves

1. Mix the two *dals* and soak in four cups of water for one hour. Drain.
2. Place the soaked *dals* in a pan with four cups of water, salt, turmeric powder, half the ginger and green chillies. Cover and cook over low heat till the *dals* are soft. Stir well with a ladle to mix the *dals* without mashing them.

3. Heat the *ghee* and butter in a *kadai*; add the cumin seeds, remaining ginger and green chillies. Stir and add the onion and sauté till light brown.

4. Add the tomatoes and sauté till the tomatoes soften. Add the chilli powder and sauté for half a minute.

5. Add the sautéed spices to the *dal* and mix well. Simmer for a few minutes and serve hot, garnished with coriander leaves.

Dal Amritsari

SUBZ LAJAWAB

15-18 French beans, cut into ½-inch pieces

3 medium carrots, cut into ½-inch pieces

2 medium green capsicums, seeded and cut into ½-inch pieces

¼ medium cauliflower, separated into small florets

3 medium potatoes, boiled, peeled and cut into ½-inch pieces

2 tablespoons oil

1 bay leaf

¾ cup boiled onion paste

2 green chillies, slit

2 teaspoons coriander powder

salt to taste

2 teaspoons red chilli powder

3 tablespoons tomato purée

½ teaspoon green cardamom powder

1. Heat the oil in a *kadai* and add the bay leaf. When it begins to change colour, add the onion paste and sauté over low heat till the oil separates. Do not brown the paste.
2. Add the green chillies, coriander powder, salt and chilli powder and sauté for two minutes. Add the tomato purée and cook for another three or four minutes.
3. Add the French beans, carrots, capsicums, cauliflower and potatoes. Cover and cook over low heat for eight to ten minutes, till vegetables are tender. Stir in the cardamom powder and serve hot.

DAL BE-AAB

¾ cup split black gram (*dhuli urad dal*)

1 teaspoon turmeric powder

1 teaspoon red chilli powder

salt to taste

⅔ cup butter

1¾ teaspoons cumin seeds

2 small onions, sliced

2 green chillies, seeded and roughly chopped

2 inches ginger, cut into thin strips

2 teaspoons *garam masala* powder

2 medium tomatoes, chopped

2 tablespoons chopped fresh coriander leaves

¼ cup lemon juice

1 teaspoon ginger paste

1 teaspoon garlic paste

1. Boil the *urad dal* in seven cups of water with turmeric powder, chilli powder and salt till done. Drain.

2. Melt half the butter in a *kadai*; add the cumin seeds and sauté till they begin to change colour. Add the onions, green chillies and ginger and sauté till the onions turn golden brown.

3. Add the cooked *dal*, lower heat and sauté for two or three minutes.

4. Add the *garam masala* powder, tomatoes, coriander leaves and lemon juice and sauté for one minute.

5. Mix the ginger paste and garlic paste with two tablespoons of water and add to the *kadai*; continue to sauté for one minute.

6. Add the remaining butter and remove from heat. Serve hot.

KADAI CHHOLAY

1½ cups chickpeas (*kabuli chana*)

salt to taste

1 tablespoon tea leaves

1-2 dried Indian gooseberries (*amla*)

5 tablespoons oil

1 tablespoon cumin seeds

1 large onion, chopped

2 tablespoons ginger paste

1 tablespoon garlic paste

1 tablespoon coriander powder

1½ teaspoons red chilli powder

½ teaspoon turmeric powder

2 teaspoons cumin powder

2 teaspoons *garam masala* powder

2-3 green chillies, slit

2 medium tomatoes, quartered

Chana Masala

1 tablespoon pomegranate seeds
   (*anardana*)

½ teaspoon cumin seeds

1 teaspoon coriander seeds

3-4 black peppercorns

½ teaspoon *kachri* powder

2 dried red chillies

Kadai Chholay

1. Soak the *kabuli chana* in three cups of water overnight, or for at least six hours.

2. Place the *chana* in a pressure cooker with three cups of water and salt. Tie the tea leaves and dried *amla* in a small piece of muslin to make a *potli* and add to the *chana*. Cook under pressure till soft. Discard the *potli*.

3. For the *chana masala*, grind all the ingredients together to a coarse paste.

4. Heat three tablespoons of oil in an iron *kadai* (*lohe ki kadai*) and add the cumin seeds. When they begin to change colour, add the onion and sauté till pink.

5. Add the ginger and garlic pastes, powdered *chana masala*, coriander powder, chilli powder, turmeric powder and half the cumin powder.

6. Add the boiled *chana* with the cooking liquid, salt, and *garam masala* powder and cook for five or six minutes.

7. In a separate pan, heat two tablespoons of oil; add the slit green chillies, remaining cumin powder and tomatoes. Cook for one minute and transfer the mixture to the *kadai*. Stir and cook over low heat till almost dry. Serve hot.

 Kadai Cooking

PANEER KHURCHAN

250 grams cottage cheese (*paneer*),
  cut into thick strips
2 tablespoons oil
1 teaspoon cumin seeds
2 teaspoons garlic paste
2 medium green capsicums,
  cut into thick strips
2 medium tomatoes, seeded and cut into
  thick strips

2 medium onions, cut into thick strips
3 tablespoons tomato purée
salt to taste
1 teaspoon red chilli powder
1 teaspoon lemon juice
1 teaspoon dried fenugreek leaves
  (*kasoori methi*), roasted and crushed

1. Heat the oil in a thick-bottomed *kadai*; add the cumin seeds. When they begin to change colour, add the garlic paste, capsicums, tomatoes and onions and sauté for five or six minutes. Add the *paneer*, tomato purée, salt and chilli powder. Sauté for a while till the *paneer* begins to stick to the pan.

2. Scrape the *paneer* off the bottom of the pan and sauté for a while longer till the *paneer* is dark brown and mashed. Stir in the lemon juice and *kasoori methi* and serve immediately.

SUBZ KHADA MASALA

½ medium bunch (125 grams) fresh fenugreek leaves (*methi*), chopped

salt to taste

10-12 French beans, chopped and blanched

½ cup shelled green peas, blanched

1 large carrot, chopped and blanched

3 medium potatoes, boiled and chopped

¼ medium cauliflower, separated into small florets, blanched

3 tablespoons oil

1 inch ginger, cut into thin strips

5-6 garlic cloves, chopped

2 medium onions, sliced

¼ teaspoon turmeric powder

½ teaspoon red chilli powder

1 medium tomato, chopped

2 green chillies, slit

1 tablespoon chopped fresh coriander leaves

1. Sprinkle a little salt on the fenugreek leaves and squeeze out the excess water after fifteen minutes.
2. Heat the oil in a *kadai*; add the ginger and garlic and sauté over medium heat for half a minute. Add the onions and sauté for half a minute longer.
3. Add the French beans, peas, carrot, potatoes and cauliflower. Stir and add the turmeric powder and chilli powder.
4. Add the tomato, green chillies and coriander leaves. Stir for a while and add the fenugreek leaves.
5. Cook over low heat till the vegetables are cooked and the water has evaporated.
6. Serve hot with *rotis*.

EKADASHI JEERA ALOO

500 grams baby potatoes, parboiled and halved

1 teaspoon cumin seeds

4 tablespoons oil

15-18 curry leaves

2 green chillies, slit

rock salt (*sendha namak*) to taste

1½ teaspoons sugar

2 tablespoons lemon juice

2 tablespoons chopped coriander leaves

3 tablespoons grated fresh coconut

1. Heat the oil in a *kadai;* add the cumin seeds, curry leaves and green chillies and sauté till they begin to change colour.
2. Add the potatoes and rock salt and sauté over medium heat for two minutes. Cover and cook over low heat till the potatoes are completely done and well browned.
3. Add the sugar, lemon juice, coriander leaves and coconut. Toss well to mix.
4. Serve hot.

 Ekadashi Jeera Aloo

MANGODI KI SABZI

200 grams *mangodi*
4 tablespoons oil
½ cup yogurt
2 tablespoons gram flour (*besan*)
salt to taste
1 teaspoon red chilli powder
1 tablespoon coriander powder
½ teaspoon turmeric powder

1 bay leaf
½ teaspoon cumin seeds
2-3 dried red chillies
½ tablespoon ginger paste
2 tablespoons tomato purée
½ teaspoon *garam masala* powder
1 tablespoon chopped fresh coriander
  leaves

1. Heat two tablespoons of oil in a *kadai* and sauté *mangodi* until crisp and slightly browned. Drain.
2. Whisk the yogurt, add the gram flour, salt, chilli powder, coriander powder and turmeric powder and mix well.
3. Heat the remaining oil in a *kadai*; add the bay leaf, cumin seeds, whole red chillies and sauté for a while.
4. Add the *mangodi*, ginger paste, tomato purée and yogurt mixture. Add one cup of water and mix well.
5. Add the *garam masala* powder and chopped coriander leaves.
6. Cook for a few minutes and serve hot.

ACHARI GOBHI

1 medium cauliflower

3 tablespoons mustard oil

½ teaspoon mustard seeds

½ teaspoon cumin seeds

¼ teaspoon fenugreek seeds (*methi dana*)

½ teaspoon fennel seeds (*saunf*)

¼ teaspoon onion seeds (*kalonji*)

1 teaspoon coriander seeds, crushed

¼ teaspoon asafoetida (*hing*)

1 medium onion, chopped

1 teaspoon ginger paste

1 teaspoon garlic paste

3 green chillies, chopped

salt to taste

½ teaspoon turmeric powder

¾ cup yogurt

1. Separate the cauliflower into large florets.
2. Heat the mustard oil to smoking point in a *kadai*; add the mustard seeds, cumin seeds, fenugreek seeds, fennel seeds, onion seeds, crushed coriander seeds and asafoetida, and sauté till they begin to change colour.
3. Add the onion and sauté till translucent. Add the ginger paste, garlic paste and green chillies and sauté till the onions turn light brown.
4. Add the cauliflower and salt and sauté over medium heat till brown.
5. Add the turmeric powder and one cup of water and cook, covered, for ten to fifteen minutes, or till cooked.
6. Add the yogurt and continue to cook till the water evaporates and the gravy coats the cauliflower. Serve hot.

KADAI CHICKEN

1 whole (600 grams) chicken, cut into 8 pieces

2 teaspoons cumin seeds

2 teaspoons coriander seeds

8 black peppercorns

5 dried red chillies

2½ tablespoons oil

1 large onion, chopped

½ tablespoon ginger paste

½ tablespoon garlic paste

2-3 green chillies, chopped

2 large tomatoes, chopped

salt to taste

¼ teaspoon *garam masala* powder

2 tablespoons chopped fresh coriander leaves

1. Dry-roast the cumin seeds, coriander seeds, peppercorns and red chillies. Cool and pound to a coarse powder.

2. Heat the oil in a *kadai;* add the onion and sauté till brown. Add the ginger paste, garlic paste and green chillies and sauté for a while.

3. Add the tomatoes and salt and cook, covered, for two minutes. Add the ground *masala* powder and sauté for one minute.

4. Add the chicken, stir, cover and cook over medium heat till the chicken is tender and the excess moisture has dried up.

5. Add the *garam masala* powder, garnish with coriander leaves and serve hot.

MURG KA MOKAL

700 grams boneless chicken breasts
4 tablespoons oil
3 medium onions, sliced
1 teaspoon cumin seeds
2 tablespoons ginger paste
2 tablespoons garlic paste
½ cup yogurt, whisked
1 teaspoon red chilli powder

½ teaspoon turmeric powder
salt to taste
2 tablespoons cashew nut paste
1 teaspoon *garam masala* powder
½ teaspoon green cardamom powder
12-15 roasted almonds, slivered

1. Cut the chicken into half-inch thick strips. Blanch in boiling water for two minutes and drain.
2. Heat the oil in a *kadai;* add the onions and sauté over medium heat till golden brown. Add the cumin seeds, stir and add the ginger paste and garlic paste mixed with four tablespoons of water. Cook for one minute and remove from heat.
3. Stir in the yogurt and return the *kadai* to the heat. Cook till the oil separates.
4. Add the chicken strips and half a cup of water; bring to a boil, lower heat and simmer till the chicken is tender.
5. Add the chilli powder, turmeric powder and salt.
6. Remove the pan from heat and stir in the cashew nut paste mixed with one-fourth cup of water.
7. Return the *kadai* to the heat and bring to a boil. Add the *garam masala* powder and cardamom powder, stir well and adjust seasoning.
8. Serve hot, garnished with roasted almond slivers.

Kadai Cooking

KADAI GOSHT HUSSAINEE

500 grams boneless mutton,
  cut into ¾-inch pieces

1 cup yogurt, whisked

1 teaspoon red chilli powder

1 teaspoon coriander powder

salt to taste

6 medium onions

2 tablespoons oil

3 inches ginger, chopped

10-12 garlic cloves, chopped

3 green chillies, slit and seeded

1¾ teaspoons cumin seeds

1¾ teaspoons mustard seeds

2½ teaspoons coriander seeds, crushed

3 tablespoons almond paste

3 tablespoons cream

a generous pinch of saffron

2 tablespoons warm milk

1 teaspoon crushed dried fenugreek leaves
  (*kasoori methi*)

½ teaspoon green cardamom powder

1 large green capsicum, cut into 1-inch
  pieces

1 large tomato, cut into 1-inch pieces

2 tablespoons chopped fresh coriander
  leaves

1. Mix together the yogurt, chilli powder, coriander powder and salt. Marinate the mutton in the mixture for at least thirty minutes, preferably in a refrigerator.

2. Slice four onions and chop the rest into one-inch cubes.

3. Heat the oil in a *kadai;* add the sliced onions and sauté over medium heat till light brown.

4. Add the ginger, garlic and green chillies. Sauté till the onions turn golden brown.

5. Add the cumin seeds, mustard seeds and crushed coriander seeds. Stir for half a minute and add the mutton with the marinade.

6. Add four cups of water, bring to a boil, cover and simmer until the mutton is tender and the excess moisture has evaporated.

7. Add the almond paste mixed with the cream, bring to a boil and lower the heat.

8. Stir in the saffron soaked in the warm milk. Sprinkle the crushed *kasoori methi* and cardamom powder. Add the onion cubes and green capsicum and stir-fry for two minutes. Add the tomato and stir-fry for one minute. Serve hot, garnished with coriander leaves.

 Kadai Gosht Hussainee

NARIAL KA GOSHT

1 kilogram leg of lamb, cut into ¾-inch pieces
1¾ cups grated fresh coconut
¾ cup oil
5 green cardamoms
1 black cardamom
5 cloves
1 inch cinnamon
1 bay leaf
1 blade of mace (*javitri*)

3 ½ teaspoons garlic paste
8 medium onions, sliced
2 inches ginger, chopped
6 green chillies, seeded and chopped
2 teaspoons red chilli powder
16-20 curry leaves, deep-fried
6 medium tomatoes, chopped
salt to taste
1 teaspoon fennel (*saunf*) powder
4 dried red chillies, cut into thin strips

1. Heat the oil in a *kadai*; add the green cardamoms, black cardamom, cloves, cinnamon, bay leaf and mace. Sauté over medium heat till fragrant.
2. Add the garlic paste and sauté for a few seconds. Add the onions and sauté until light brown. Add the ginger and green chillies and continue to sauté until the onions turn golden brown.
3. Add the chilli powder, one cup of grated coconut and the curry leaves.
4. Sauté for one minute and add the tomatoes and salt. Cook, stirring continuously, till the oil separates.
5. Add the lamb and sauté for five minutes. Add three-and-a-half cups of water and bring to a boil. Lower heat, cover and simmer until the lamb is tender and the liquid has evaporated. Adjust seasoning.
6. Sprinkle fennel powder and stir. Transfer to a bowl and garnish with red chilli strips and remaining grated coconut. Serve hot.

Main Course - Non-Vegetarian

DAHI KA KEEMA

700 grams minced mutton (*keema*)

1⅓ cups yogurt, whisked

2 tablespoons oil

3 green cardamoms

1 black cardamom

5 cloves

1 inch cinnamon

1 bay leaf

1 blade of mace (*javitri*)

2 medium onions, finely chopped

2 teaspoons ginger paste

2 teaspoons garlic paste

2 teaspoons red chilli powder

salt to taste

3 tablespoons chopped fresh coriander leaves

10 green chillies, seeded and deep-fried

1. Heat the oil in a *kadai*; add the green cardamoms, black cardamom, cloves, cinnamon, bay leaf and mace. Sauté over medium heat till fragrant.
2. Add the onions and sauté till brown. Add the ginger paste and garlic paste mixed with a quarter cup of water, and sauté for half a minute.
3. Add the chilli powder and salt and sauté for two minutes.
4. Add the *keema* and sauté till dry. Add the yogurt, bring to a boil, cover and simmer until the *keema* is cooked.
5. Add half the coriander leaves and deep-fried green chillies.
6. Stir well and transfer to a serving bowl. Garnish with the remaining coriander leaves and deep-fried green chillies.
7. Serve hot with *roti*.

SURMAI WITH TOMATOES

4 (100 grams each) one-inch thick *surmai* fillets

3 medium tomatoes, chopped

3 tablespoons oil

salt to taste

black pepper powder to taste

1 large onion, chopped

4 garlic cloves, crushed

1 teaspoon coriander powder

1 teaspoon roasted cumin powder

½ teaspoon turmeric powder

1½ teaspoons red chilli powder

¾ cup coconut milk

½ teaspoon *garam masala* powder

2 tablespoons chopped fresh coriander leaves

 Surmai with Tomatoes

1. Heat the oil in a large shallow *kadai* and add the fish fillets. Season with salt and pepper powder and fry for two minutes on each side. Drain and keep warm.

2. To the same *kadai,* add the onion and sauté till light golden brown. Add the garlic and sauté for half a minute.

3. Add the tomatoes and salt and cook, covered, till the tomatoes are soft and pulpy. Add the coriander powder, roasted cumin powder, turmeric powder and chilli powder and continue to sauté for two minutes.

4. Stir in the coconut milk and adjust seasoning. Add the *garam masala* powder and coriander leaves and mix well.

5. Add the fried fish, stir gently and serve.

GOSHT GULBARGA

600 grams boneless lamb, cut into 1-inch cubes

6 cloves

¼ teaspoon green cardamom seeds

1 tablespoon cumin seeds

2 inches cinnamon

¼ teaspoon grated nutmeg

2 tablespoons coriander seeds

2 tablespoons ginger paste

2 tablespoons garlic paste

salt to taste

4 tablespoons oil

2 bay leaves

2 large onions, chopped

1 tablespoon red chilli powder

¼ teaspoon turmeric powder

3 tablespoons coconut paste

3 tablespoons cashew nut paste

2 tablespoons chopped fresh coriander leaves

1. Dry-roast the cloves, cardamom seeds, cumin seeds, cinnamon, nutmeg and coriander seeds in a *kadai*. Cool and grind to a powder.

2. Mix together the *masala* powder, half the ginger and garlic pastes, salt and one tablespoon of oil. Marinate the lamb in the mixture for one hour, preferably in a refrigerator.

3. Heat the remaining oil in the same *kadai*; add the bay leaves and onions and sauté till the onions turn golden brown.

4. Add the remaining ginger paste and garlic paste and continue to stir over high heat for one minute.

5. Add the chilli powder, turmeric powder and marinated lamb. Add two cups of water and cook over low heat for one hour, or till the lamb is almost cooked.

6. Add the coconut paste and cashew nut paste and continue to simmer for fifteen to twenty minutes, or till the lamb is tender.

7. Transfer to a serving bowl and garnish with coriander leaves. Serve hot.

KEKDA CURRY

8 small crabs

4 onions

7 tablespoons oil

12-15 black peppercorns

1 tablespoon coriander seeds

12 dried red chillies

½ teaspoon caraway seeds (*shahi jeera*)

½ teaspoon green cardamom seeds

8 cloves

2 inches cinnamon

4 tablespoons tamarind pulp

2 tablespoons grated fresh coconut

¼ teaspoon turmeric powder

salt to taste

1 cup coconut milk

2 tablespoons chopped fresh coriander leaves

1. Chop the crabs into bite-size pieces. Slice two of the onions and chop the rest.
2. In a *kadai*, lightly roast the peppercorns, coriander seeds, red chillies, caraway seeds, cardamom seeds, cloves and cinnamon.

3. Add two tablespoons of oil to the *kadai* and fry the sliced onions till brown. Drain on absorbent paper. Grind the fried onions with the tamarind pulp and roasted spices to a smooth paste.

4. Add two more tablespoons of oil to the same *kadai* and sauté the coconut with turmeric powder. Cool and grind to a paste.

5. Add the remaining oil to the *kadai* and sauté the chopped onions. Add the crabs and salt and cook for five or six minutes, stirring frequently.

6. Add the *masala* paste and coconut paste. Stir well and add three-fourth cup of water. Bring to a boil, lower heat and simmer for five minutes. Stir in the coconut milk. Cook over medium heat till the gravy thickens.

7. Serve hot, garnished with coriander leaves.

 Kekda Curry

KADAI PRAWNS

40 (600 grams) medium prawns, peeled
  and deveined
2 teaspoons cumin seeds
2 teaspoons coriander seeds
8 black peppercorns
5 dried red chillies
2 tablespoons oil
1 inch ginger, cut into thin strips
2 green chillies, cut into thin strips

2 medium onions, chopped
1/4 cup chopped fresh coriander leaves
2 medium tomatoes, chopped
6 tablespoons tomato purée
salt to taste
1/2 teaspoon sugar
2 teaspoons lemon juice
1/2 teaspoon *garam masala* powder

1. Dry-roast the cumin seeds, coriander seeds, peppercorns and red chillies. Cool and pound to a coarse powder.
2. Heat the oil in a *kadai*. Add the ginger and green chillies and sauté for half a minute. Add the onions and sauté till light brown.
3. Add the *masala* powder, half the coriander leaves, the tomatoes, tomato purée, salt, sugar and lemon juice, and cook till the oil separates.
4. Add the prawns with half cup of water and cook over medium heat for seven to eight minutes. Sprinkle the *garam masala* powder and serve hot, garnished with the remaining coriander leaves.

METHI MURG

1 whole (800 grams) chicken, cut into 8 pieces

¼ small bunch (75 grams) fresh fenugreek leaves (*methi*), chopped

1 cup yogurt, whisked

salt to taste

4 inches ginger

3 tablespoons oil

5 green cardamoms

1 black cardamom

5 cloves

1 inch cinnamon

1 bay leaf

1-2 blades of mace (*javitri*)

2 large onions, chopped

20 garlic cloves, chopped

3 green chillies, seeded and chopped

½ teaspoon turmeric powder

1 teaspoon coriander powder

1 teaspoon red chilli powder

2 medium tomatoes, chopped

1 tablespoon dried fenugreek leaves (*kasoori methi*)

3 tablespoons chopped fresh coriander leaves

1. Mix together the yogurt and salt in a large bowl. Add the chicken and leave to marinate for about half an hour. Chop half the ginger and cut the rest into thin strips.

2. Heat the oil in a *kadai*; add the green and black cardamoms, cloves, cinnamon, bay leaf and mace and sauté for one minute. Add the onions and sauté till golden brown. Add the chopped ginger, garlic and green chillies and cook for two minutes.

3. Stir in the turmeric powder, coriander powder, chilli powder and one-fourth cup of water and cook for half a minute. Add the tomatoes and cook till soft.

4. Add the marinated chicken and fenugreek leaves and mix well. Cover and cook over medium heat till the chicken is tender.

5. Sprinkle the ginger strips, *kasoori methi* and coriander leaves over the chicken. Cover and leave to stand for about five minutes before serving.

MAKAI PALAK PULAO

1¼ cups Basmati rice

¾ cup corn kernels (*makai*), blanched

2 medium bunches (500 grams) fresh
   spinach leaves (*palak*), chopped

1½ teaspoons oil

1 teaspoon cumin seeds

1 bay leaf

2 cloves

5 black peppercorns

2 green cardamoms

2 black cardamoms

1 inch cinnamon

1 blade mace (*javitri*)

1 inch ginger, chopped

4-6 garlic cloves, chopped

2-3 green chillies, slit

salt to taste

1 tablespoon lemon juice

1 teaspoon *garam masala* powder

1. Soak the rice in three cups of water for half an hour. Drain and cook in four cups of water till three-fourth done. Drain.

2. Heat the oil in a non-stick *kadai*. Add the cumin seeds and when they begin to change colour, add the bay leaf, cloves, peppercorns, green and black cardamoms, cinnamon and mace. Stir-fry till fragrant.

3. Add the ginger, garlic and green chillies. Cook over medium heat for one minute.

4. Add the corn and continue cooking for two or three minutes. Add the spinach and rice, and cook, stirring gently for about a minute.

5. Add the salt, lemon juice and *garam masala* powder and stir. Lower heat, cover the *kadai* and continue cooking for about five to seven minutes, or till the rice is completely cooked.

6. Serve hot.

CHICKEN KEEMA PULAO

200 grams minced chicken (*keema*)

¾ cup Basmati rice, soaked

2½ tablespoons oil

2 medium onions, sliced

salt to taste

1 teaspoon red chilli powder

¼ teaspoon turmeric powder

¼ cup yogurt

1 teaspoon *garam masala* powder

½ teaspoon cumin seeds

5-6 garlic cloves, chopped

1 inch ginger, chopped

2 green cardamoms

2 cloves

1 inch cinnamon

5 black peppercorns

3 green chillies, slit

2 tablespoons chopped fresh mint leaves

2 tablespoons chopped fresh coriander leaves

1. Boil the rice in two cups of water. Drain.

2. Heat half the oil in a *kadai*; add the onions and sauté till light golden brown. Add the chicken mince and continue to sauté for two or three minutes.

3. Add the salt, chilli powder and turmeric powder and cook, covered, for two minutes.

4. Add the yogurt and half a cup of water and continue to cook till the mince is tender. Stir in the *garam masala* powder.

5. Heat the remaining oil in a separate *kadai*; add the cumin seeds and when they begin to change colour, add the garlic, ginger, cardamoms, cloves, cinnamon, peppercorns and green chillies and sauté for one minute.

6. Add the cooked chicken mince and stir in the rice. Add the mint leaves and coriander leaves and toss to mix well.

7. Serve hot.

Kadai Cooking

CHUTNEY PULAO

1½ cups Basmati rice, cooked

2 tablespoons chopped fresh coriander leaves

1 tablespoon chopped fresh mint leaves

5-6 green chillies

10-15 garlic cloves

2½ tablespoons oil

½ teaspoon cumin seeds

2 dried red chillies, broken into bits

1 inch cinnamon

5 cloves

1 bay leaf

1 large onion, sliced

½ cup shelled green peas

150 grams cottage cheese (*paneer*), cut into ½-inch cubes

salt to taste

10 baby potatoes, boiled and halved

2 tablespoons lemon juice

1. Grind together the coriander leaves, mint leaves, green chillies and garlic to a fine paste.
2. Heat the oil in a *kadai*; add the cumin seeds, red chillies, cinnamon, cloves and bay leaf and sauté for one minute.
3. Add the onion and sauté for one minute. Add the ground paste, green peas, *paneer*, salt and potatoes and sauté for two minutes.
4. Add the rice and lemon juice and mix well. Serve hot.

 Kadai Cooking

PHODNICHA BHAAT

2 cups cooked rice

2 tablespoons oil

½ teaspoon mustard seeds

½ teaspoon cumin seeds

6 curry leaves

2 green chillies, finely chopped

¼ teaspoon turmeric powder

¼ teaspoon red chilli powder

1 medium onion, finely chopped

¼ cup roasted peanuts, crushed

1 tablespoon lemon juice

salt to taste

¼ teaspoon sugar

2 tablespoons chopped fresh coriander leaves

1. Heat the oil in a *kadai*; add the mustard seeds, cumin seeds, curry leaves and green chillies and stir till the seeds begin to splutter.

2. Add the turmeric powder and chilli powder and sauté, making sure that the *masala* does not burn. Add the onion and sauté till translucent.

3. Add the rice and stir-fry till the *masala* is mixed well into the rice. Add the peanuts.

4. Sprinkle some water over the rice and cook, covered, for one minute over low heat. Stir in the lemon juice, salt and sugar.

5. Serve immediately, garnished with coriander leaves.

Kadai Cooking

MOONG DAL HALWA

1 cup split green gram (*dhuli moong dal*)
1 cup sugar
a generous pinch of saffron
½ cup milk

1 cup pure *ghee*
¾ cup *khoya/mawa*, crumbled
10-12 almonds, blanched and slivered

1. Soak the *moong dal* for six hours. Grind coarsely with very little water.
2. Prepare a sugar syrup of one-string consistency with sugar and one-and-a-half cups of water. Soak the saffron in hot milk.
3. Heat the *ghee* in a thick-bottomed *kadai* and add the ground *moong dal*. Cook, stirring continuously, over low heat till golden brown. Add the sugar syrup and saffron milk. Cook, stirring continuously, till well mixed and the *halwa* is of dropping consistency. Add the *khoya* and cook till it melts. Serve hot, decorated with almond slivers.

Chef's tip: Add 1 tablespoon of *besan* to the melted *ghee* before adding the *dal*.

Desserts

SOOJI AUR BADAM KA HALWA

½ cup semolina (*rawa/sooji*), roasted

2 cups almonds

6 tablespoons pure *ghee*

1½ cups sugar

2 cups milk

a few saffron threads

½ teaspoon green cardamom powder

1. Roast the almonds. Reserve eight to ten for garnishing and coarsely powder the rest.
2. Heat the *ghee* in a *kadai* and roast the semolina till light brown. Add the almond powder and continue to sauté for two or three minutes.
3. Add the sugar, milk and saffron. Cook over medium heat, stirring continuously, till the sugar dissolves and the mixture attains the consistency of *halwa*.
4. Add the cardamom powder and mix well. Remove from heat, decorate with the reserved almonds and serve hot.

KALAKAND

2 litres milk
¼ teaspoon alum (*phitkari*), crushed
4 tablespoons sugar

½ tablespoon *ghee*
15-20 pistachios, thinly sliced
silver *varq*

1. Boil the milk in a large, thick-bottomed *kadai* till it thickens slightly. Add the alum (*phitkari*) to the thickened milk and stir continuously till the milk becomes grainy. Cook till most of the moisture evaporates and a solid mass remains.

2. Add the sugar and mix well. Cook for five or ten minutes longer till the mixture thickens again.

3. Grease an aluminium tray with *ghee*. Pour the milk mixture into the tray and level the surface. Sprinkle the sliced pistachios on top. Leave to set for a few hours in a cool, dry place. When completely set, decorate with silver *varq* and cut into squares or diamonds. Consume immediatly as it does not keep for long.

SAEB KA HALWA

2 cups grated apples
¾ cup sugar
½ cup *khoya/mawa*, grated

¼ teaspoon green cardamom powder
2 tablespoons chopped mixed nuts

1. **Cook** the grated apples with sugar in a thick-bottomed *kadai* till the sugar melts.
2. **Add** the *khoya* and cook over low heat until the *khoya* melts.
3. **Continue** to cook over low heat, stirring continuously, until the moisture dries up. Stir in the cardamom powder.
4. **Decorate** with the mixed nuts and serve hot.